NEW ENGLAND WHALER

BY ROBERT F. BALDWIN

ILLUSTRATIONS BY RICHARD ERICKSON

LERNER PUBLICATIONS COMPANY
MINNEAPOLIS, MINNESOTA

The American Pastfinder series is produced by Lerner Publications Company
in cooperation with Greenleaf Publishing, Inc., St. Charles, Illinois.

Design by Melanie Lawson

Baldwin, Robert F.
    New England Whaler / by Robert F. Baldwin; illustrations by Richard
Erickson.
        p. cm. — (American Pastfinder)
    Includes index.
    Summary: Surveys the New England whaling industry in the 1700s and
1800s, describing the ships that were used, daily life and traditions of the
whalers, the dangers they faced, and more.
    ISBN 0-8225-2978-5 (alk. paper)
    1. Whaling—New England—History—Juvenile literature.
[1. Whaling—New England—History.] I. Erickson, Richard (Richard W.),
ill. II. Title. III. Series.
SH383.2.B34 1996
638.2'8—dc20   95-14542

Manufactured in the United States of America
1 2 3 4 5 6 - H - 01 00 99 98 97 96

CONTENTS

Introduction...5

The Whale Hunters..6

"Greasy Luck" 8

Those Magnificent Creatures 11

Ugly Lump of a Ship 12

Fitting Out 14

A Working Crew 16

Life at Sea 18

Plum Duff and Monkey Jackets................................21

The Harpooner and His Weapons 22

"There Blows!"..25

Cutting In 26

Trying Out 28

Families at Sea...30

Trapped in the Ice..32

The Tragedy of the Whaling Ship Essex 34

Homeward Bound..37

Scrimshaw...38

End of an Era 40

Whaler Recipes..42

Whaling Song 43

True-Life Whalers 44

Whaling Terms and Their Meanings 46

Index 47

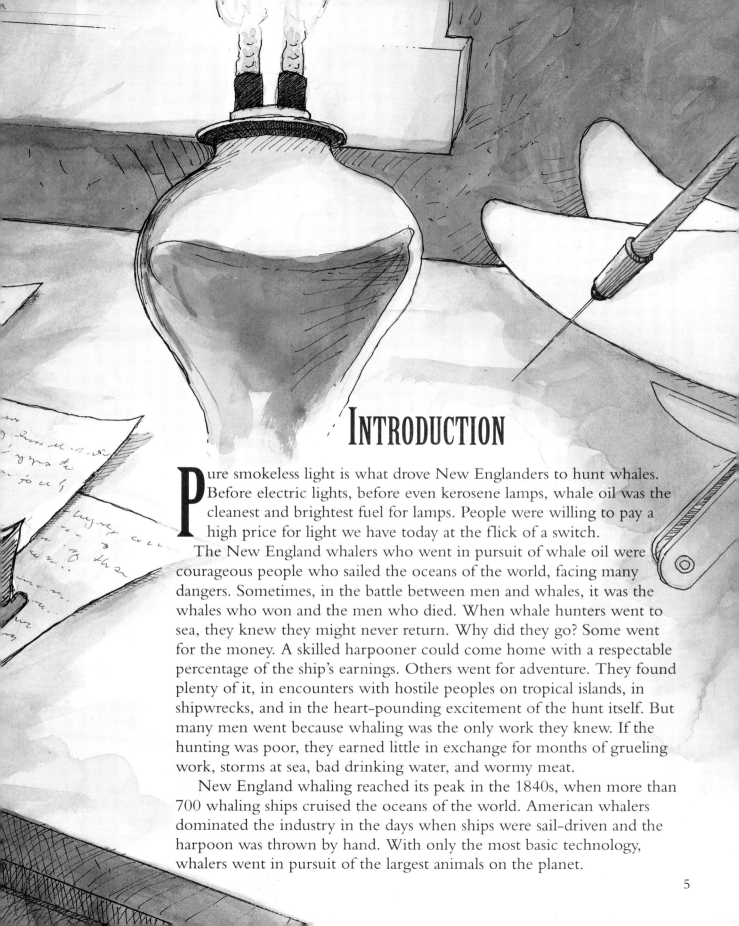

INTRODUCTION

Pure smokeless light is what drove New Englanders to hunt whales. Before electric lights, before even kerosene lamps, whale oil was the cleanest and brightest fuel for lamps. People were willing to pay a high price for light we have today at the flick of a switch.

The New England whalers who went in pursuit of whale oil were courageous people who sailed the oceans of the world, facing many dangers. Sometimes, in the battle between men and whales, it was the whales who won and the men who died. When whale hunters went to sea, they knew they might never return. Why did they go? Some went for the money. A skilled harpooner could come home with a respectable percentage of the ship's earnings. Others went for adventure. They found plenty of it, in encounters with hostile peoples on tropical islands, in shipwrecks, and in the heart-pounding excitement of the hunt itself. But many men went because whaling was the only work they knew. If the hunting was poor, they earned little in exchange for months of grueling work, storms at sea, bad drinking water, and wormy meat.

New England whaling reached its peak in the 1840s, when more than 700 whaling ships cruised the oceans of the world. American whalers dominated the industry in the days when ships were sail-driven and the harpoon was thrown by hand. With only the most basic technology, whalers went in pursuit of the largest animals on the planet.

5

THE WHALE HUNTERS

For thousands of years, people living near the ocean have hunted whales. Inuit tribes killed whales for meat. Europeans along the coast of France and Spain hunted them too, mainly for their oil and for certain kinds of whalebone. When Europeans began exploring the coast of New England, they saw Native American hunters attacking whales. The Native Americans hunted close to shore from their canoes, using bows and arrows and spears.

European settlers on America's east coast also hunted whales near shore. In the 1640s, colonists on Long Island turned shore-based whaling into a regular business and hired Native Americans to help them. Using small but sturdy boats, they hunted a species known as the "right whale." It produced plenty of oil, swam slowly, came close to shore, and floated after it was killed. For those reasons, the colonists considered it the "right" kind of whale to hunt. After killing a whale, the hunters towed it ashore where they cut the blubber, or fat, from the whale and melted it into oil. This kind of whaling spread to Connecticut, Cape Cod, and the Massachusetts islands of Martha's Vineyard and Nantucket. Shore-based whale hunting killed so many right whales that by the early 1700s they had become hard to find.

Whaling on the Open Sea

In about 1712, a small Nantucket sloop filled with whale hunters ventured farther out to sea than usual. As a storm approached, the whale hunters encountered a school of sperm whales. Despite the storm and the fierce fighting abilities of this species, the men killed one whale. The news spread fast. Sperm whales, although smaller than right whales, could be found in abundance on the high seas. From that day forward, Nantucket ships began venturing farther offshore in search of sperm whales.

The town of Nantucket (on Nantucket Island) soon became the most important whaling port in New England. The owners of Nantucket whaling ships grew rich. Larger ships were built to hold more oil. Sometimes they came home so heavy with barrels of oil that they could no longer pass through the shallow entrance to Nantucket's harbor. Eventually, New Bedford, Massachusetts, a deepwater port, became the whaling capital of the world.

Hardships and Dangers

American whalers shipped out on long voyages knowing that they might drown or be killed by a wounded whale. There were other dangers and hardships as well. When whale carcasses were being cut up, men worked to the point of exhaustion, in good weather and in bad, on heaving decks made slippery with the oil and blood of whales.

Sailors often fell and suffered serious injuries, sometimes gashing themselves with their razor-sharp cutting tools. When they were injured, there was no doctor to set their broken bones or stitch their wounds. In most cases, the captain patched up the men as best he could, using medical knowledge he had picked up from books and through experience.

Illness took its toll as well. Sailors were sometimes stricken with scurvy, a disease caused by diets lacking in fresh fruits and vegetables. Victims of pneumonia, appendicitis, and other illnesses were often buried at sea.

The safety of the ship and its crew depended on close cooperation and obedience to rules. Any misbehavior was dealt with severely. Until 1850, when laws were enacted to protect seamen from cruel treatment, captains punished crew members by having them whipped. Seamen often rebelled against this kind of harsh treatment and ran away when the ship reached a foreign port. Occasionally, crew members banded together in rebellion against the captain and officers. During one such mutiny, a Nantucket whaler named Samuel Comstock murdered the captain and all the officers aboard the whaling ship *Globe*. Then he took command of the ship and found a tropical island where he tried to set himself up as a king. He was killed there by some of his former shipmates.

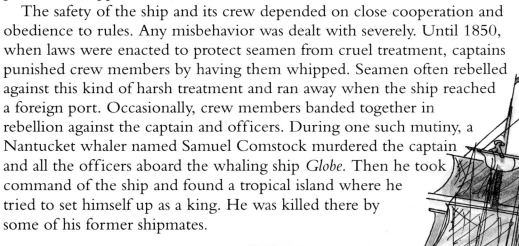

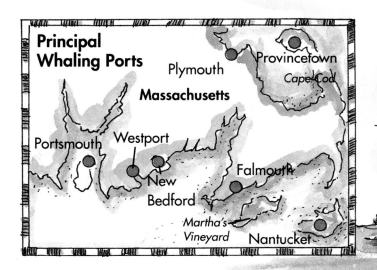

Principal Whaling Ports

Plymouth

Provincetown

Cape Cod

Massachusetts

Portsmouth

Westport

Falmouth

New Bedford

Martha's Vineyard

Nantucket

"Greasy Luck"

Harpooners and sailors from Nantucket and New Bedford roamed the oceans of the earth, wherever whales might be found. Whalers regularly crossed the Atlantic and Pacific Oceans and hunted whales from the warm waters of the Indian Ocean to the icy waters of the Arctic.

Everybody on board a whaling ship hoped for what whale hunters called "greasy luck"—a voyage ending with a ship filled with barrels of whale oil and profits for all.

To Each a Share

Most of the profits of the voyage belonged to the ship owners, but each member of the crew received a share of the money called a "lay." The size of a crew member's lay depended on his skill, experience, and rank in the crew. The captain's lay was the largest. The cabin boy's was the smallest.

A successful trip produced tens of thousands of dollars for the owners. The captain, the officers, and the harpooners made good money too, but ordinary seamen seldom did. Crew members had to pay for their clothing and other gear, and that cost was deducted from each man's lay. An ordinary seaman might finish a voyage with only one or two hundred dollars for four years of hard, dangerous work.

The Quest for Adventure

Although they didn't get rich, crew members had adventures and saw sights that most Americans couldn't even begin to imagine. They watched the dances of Polynesian islanders and saw the morning sunlight strike the peak of Mount Fuji in Japan. Their ports of call included Russian villages in the Aleutian Islands, sun-drenched islands in the South Pacific, and fishing villages along the coast of Africa. Above all, there was the excitement and thrill of doing battle with an enormous creature so powerful it could smash a boat into splinters with a flick of its mighty tail.

bowhead

pilot

gray

right

fin

killer

humpback

beluga
or white

beaked

sperm

blue

THOSE MAGNIFICENT CREATURES

Whales can be found in all the oceans of the world. Although they spend their entire lives in the sea, whales are mammals. Some can stay underwater for 30 to 50 minutes, but eventually they must return to the surface for air. When they do, their breath bursts forth from blowholes on their heads.

There are more than 75 different kinds of whales alive in the world today. They are divided into two groups, baleen whales and toothed whales.

Baleen Whales

Baleen whales were the first whales to be hunted commercially. Instead of teeth, these whales have rows of fringed plates in their mouths. The whales use these plates, or baleen, to strain tiny plants and animals, called plankton, from the sea. Baleen, sometimes called whalebone, is a springy, somewhat flexible material that was often made into stiffeners for clothing or light springs for machinery.

One species of baleen whale, the blue whale, is the largest animal that has ever lived on our planet. Some blue whales are 100 feet long and weigh as much as 140 tons. Other well-known baleen whales are the gray whale, the right whale, the bowhead whale, the fin whale, and the humpback whale.

Toothed Whales

Whales with teeth are predators that feed on fish, squid, and other sea creatures. There are about 65 kinds of toothed whales, including killer whales, pilot whales, beaked whales, beluga or white whales, and sperm whales. (Scientists include porpoises and dolphins in this group, though these mammals aren't commonly thought of as whales.) The sperm whale is a fierce fighter, with sharp teeth for catching and chewing its main source of food, the giant squid. Whale hunters had good reason to fear this whale's powerful jaws and mighty tail.

ship's wheel

overhead compass

skylight

second mate's cabin

pantry

captain's cabin

first mate's cabin

Ugly Lump of a Ship

A whaling ship, also called a whaler, was built more as a floating factory and warehouse than as a sailing ship. Its prow (front) was blunt and its sides bulged to hold as many barrels as possible. Clipper ships were prettier, but the whalers had a sturdy style all their own.

A whaling ship was the sturdiest ship afloat, made for hard work on long ocean voyages. Perhaps it was that sturdiness that gave it the label, an "ugly lump of a ship." Its hull was sheathed in copper to guard against wood-boring shipworms. If the ship was bound for Arctic waters, the hull had an extra layer of cedar planking. The business of cutting and hacking whale blubber took its toll, so, before every voyage, a whaling ship got a new wooden deck.

The first tip-offs that a ship was a whaler were the long white whaling boats, or whaleboats, suspended above the rail. As sleek as the whaling ship

blacksmith's forge

mast

ship's bell

carpenter's bench

tryworks

hatch

cooperage

galley

crew's quarters

stone ballast for balance

oil barrels

was bulky, these boats hung from curved wooden brackets. But the most unusual feature of a whaler was the "tryworks" on its deck. The tryworks was a brick furnace, housing huge cast-iron pans for cooking blubber. Cooking released the whale oil. Often, a "duck pen," a shallow tank of water beneath the furnace, protected the deck from heat. At night, the glow of the tryworks could be seen many miles away. Near the tryworks was a large opening in the railing surrounded by a plank scaffold. Sailors stood on the scaffold to cut and hoist away strips of blubber.

The ship was easy to handle, as sailing ships went. When a whale was sighted, as few as six men could deal with the sails and rigging while everyone else joined the chase. At sea, the ship was like a self-sufficient village with its own carpenter and blacksmith. It often had a farm of sorts, with pigs, goats, and chickens penned on deck.

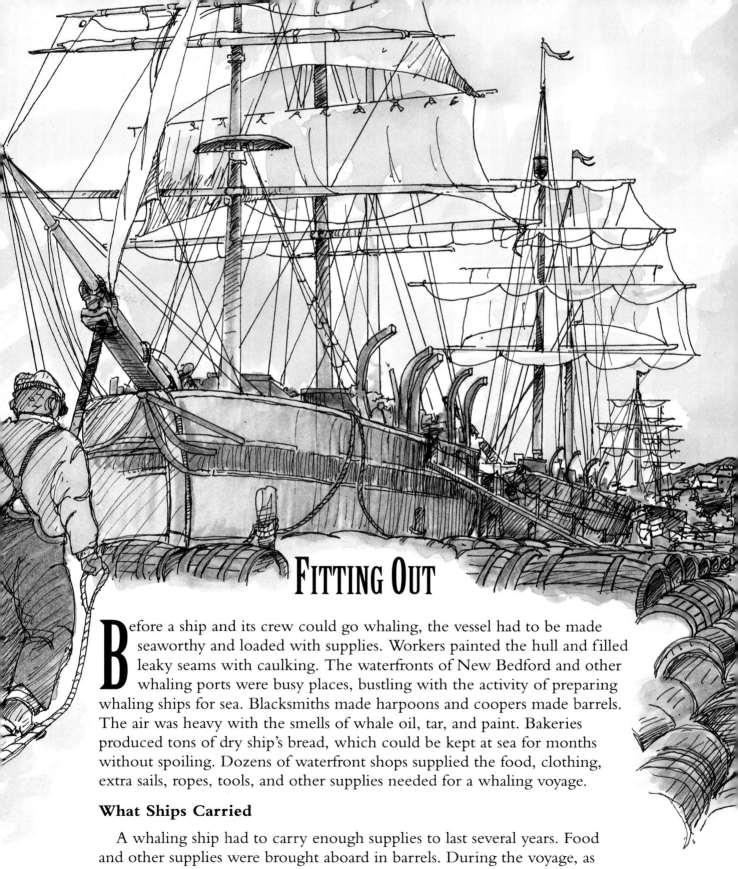

FITTING OUT

Before a ship and its crew could go whaling, the vessel had to be made seaworthy and loaded with supplies. Workers painted the hull and filled leaky seams with caulking. The waterfronts of New Bedford and other whaling ports were busy places, bustling with the activity of preparing whaling ships for sea. Blacksmiths made harpoons and coopers made barrels. The air was heavy with the smells of whale oil, tar, and paint. Bakeries produced tons of dry ship's bread, which could be kept at sea for months without spoiling. Dozens of waterfront shops supplied the food, clothing, extra sails, ropes, tools, and other supplies needed for a whaling voyage.

What Ships Carried

A whaling ship had to carry enough supplies to last several years. Food and other supplies were brought aboard in barrels. During the voyage, as

they were emptied, the barrels were used to store whale oil. Ships also carried thousands of wooden staves (strips) and iron hoops from which more barrels could be made as needed.

Most whaling ships carried three or four whaleboats and enough lumber to repair or rebuild them if they were wrecked by a whale. Each whaleboat needed oars for rowing and steering, harpoons and lances for attacking and killing whales, wooden tubs filled with harpoon line, a compass, drinking water, and dozens of other items.

A fully rigged ship could fly as many as 20 sails, but it carried more than twice that number to replace sails that might be damaged or blown away in storms. Not until all of these items had been purchased, brought aboard, and stored in their proper places was a whaling ship ready to go to sea.

A Working Crew

Whaling ships usually went to sea with a crew of more than two dozen people, including a cabin boy. The head of the ship was the captain. He had to be a strong leader and a man of sound judgment because the safety of the crew, the ship, and its precious cargo of whale oil all depended on his decisions. He had a cabin of his own, with a compass suspended over his bunk, so that even when he was resting he could tell at a glance if the ship was on course.

A ship usually had three or four officers, also known as mates. Officers ate with the captain, and when whales were sighted, each officer was in command of a whaleboat. The highest paid and most skilled of the officers was the first mate. If the captain became ill or disabled, he took over.

Skilled Trades

After the officers came the harpooners, also called boat steerers. Their lay was usually about twice the amount of an ordinary seaman's. Each ship also needed a blacksmith to make and repair iron tools, a cooper to make barrels, and a carpenter to repair damaged whaleboats and other equipment. These tradesmen earned less than a boat steerer but more than a seaman.

Other Crew Members

A ship usually carried a crew of about 16 seamen. Together they did all the manual labor of sailing a fully rigged ship. They raised and lowered the sails by pulling together on lines called halyards. They climbed into the rigging to furl, or gather in, the canvas sails. They took turns as lookouts on the mainmast, and when whales were sighted, they manned the oars in the whaleboats. After a whale was killed, the crew cut away the blubber, melted it in the tryworks, and stored the whale oil in barrels. The cook prepared meals. The steward was in charge of the ship's provisions and served meals to the officers. The cabin boy did errands and assisted the steward and cook.

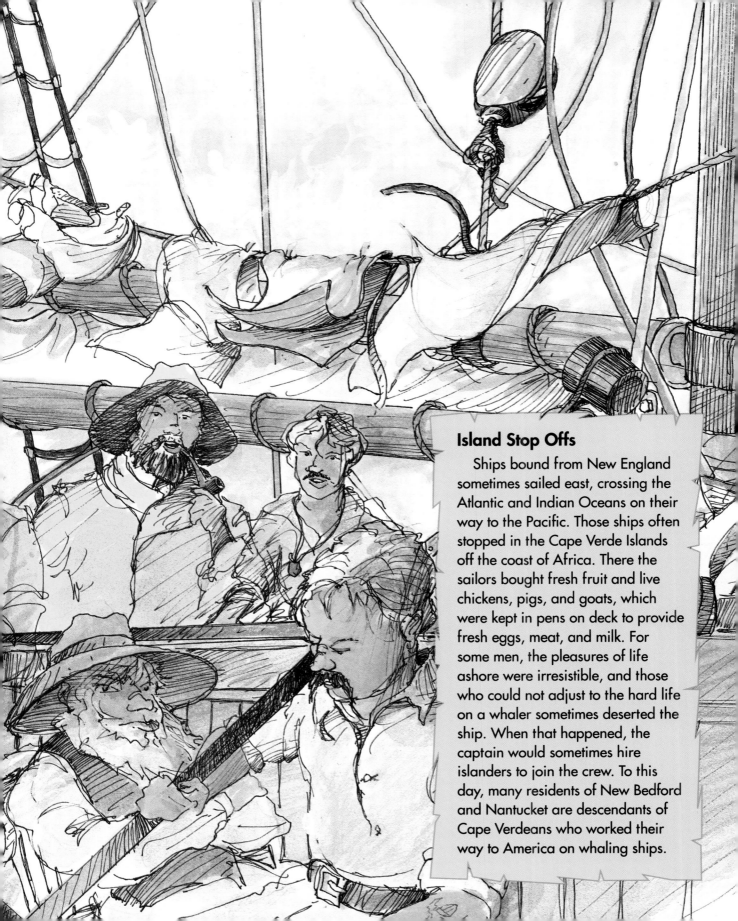

Island Stop Offs

Ships bound from New England sometimes sailed east, crossing the Atlantic and Indian Oceans on their way to the Pacific. Those ships often stopped in the Cape Verde Islands off the coast of Africa. There the sailors bought fresh fruit and live chickens, pigs, and goats, which were kept in pens on deck to provide fresh eggs, meat, and milk. For some men, the pleasures of life ashore were irresistible, and those who could not adjust to the hard life on a whaler sometimes deserted the ship. When that happened, the captain would sometimes hire islanders to join the crew. To this day, many residents of New Bedford and Nantucket are descendants of Cape Verdeans who worked their way to America on whaling ships.

LIFE AT SEA

Life at sea wasn't always exciting or even busy. Whaling ships had large crews, and, except when whales were sighted, there wasn't always much for the men to do. A seaman would take his turn steering the ship or watching for whales from the top of the mainmast. He would spend an hour or two a day doing chores like scrubbing the decks or bringing supplies from the hold. The rest of the time he was free to do as he pleased.

In the Forecastle

Ordinary crew members slept in the forecastle, a compartment in the forward part of the ship. With 15 to 20 men living there, the forecastle was a crowded place, filled with the smells of tobacco, damp clothing, and sweat. There, men read, slept, and played backgammon, a board game that was extremely popular in the 19th century.

During cold weather, crew members gathered in the forecastle to talk and entertain each other with stories and songs. Sometimes they told of their seagoing adventures on other ships or made up fanciful tales to impress or scare newcomers. They sang hymns, popular songs of the day, and songs about the sea. Some played musical instruments like the fiddle or concertina.

"Gams" Brought News from Home

Meeting another Yankee (New England) whaling ship at sea was always a welcome break. This visit was called a "gam" and offered whalers the chance to exchange news, letters, books, and newspapers. If the other ship was on its way home, letters could be sent to loved ones. Sometimes the other ship was outward-bound with news from home. Sometimes a gam would last several days while the captains compared notes and planned their ongoing search for whales.

Time on the Ship

Time was measured in "watches." The day was divided into five watches of four hours each, plus two "dog watches" of two hours each. Each half hour was rung out during the watch, with one ring of the bell for the first half hour, two for the second, on through eight bells for the end of the watch. During any watch, half the crew would be on duty while the other half was free to relax.

watch 6

watch 1

24
midnight

dog watch

dog watch

18

6

watch 2

12
noon

watch 4

watch 3

bells

Inside the Slop Chest

In 1858, the whaling ship *Florida* carried these items in its slop (storage) chest for a three-year voyage:

20 extra-heavy jackets	2 dozen neck comforters
26 jackets	3 dozen Russian caps
72 pairs of trousers	belts
15 red flannel shirts	knives and sheaths
60 Saint Kersey shirts	needles
40 cotton shirts	yarn
5 dozen fancy calico shirts	boots
75 undershirts	shoes
6 dozen socks	slippers
7½ dozen stockings	hats
4 dozen mittens	tobacco
1 dozen heavy frocks	cigars
4 dozen denim frocks	spoons
75 pairs of underwear	pots and pans

PLUM DUFF AND MONKEY JACKETS

The food and clothing of whalers were determined by the nature of their work. Whaling ships carried food that would last for a long time without spoiling. As for clothing, whalers needed garments to keep them comfortable and dry in many climates and all kinds of weather.

What Whale Hunters Ate

The first few days after leaving a port, the crew ate fresh meat, vegetables, and fruit. But there was no way to keep food fresh. Most meals were built around food that had been preserved by drying or salting.

Meals included lots of salted beef, pork, and codfish; beans, rice, potatoes, dry ship's bread, and dried fruit. The best food was served to the captain, officers, and harpooners. Seamen ate lots of salted beef, which they called "salt junk." On special occasions, they ate "lobscouse," a hash made from salted meat and hard bread. The biggest treat was plum duff, a dessert made with dried fruit.

What Whalers Wore

Crew members wore short, wool "monkey jackets" in cold weather, but they also needed lightweight shirts and pants for the tropics and waterproof boots, work clothes, and "sou'wester" rain hats to keep them dry in rough seas and storms.

Every whaling port had plenty of outfitters to supply these items. The sailors called these eager merchants "land sharks," because they sent salesmen along the waterfront looking for customers. A sailor buying gear for a voyage didn't need cash. The cost was paid by the ship owners and subtracted from the sailor's lay at the end of the voyage. If a sailor needed more clothing at sea, he could buy it from the ship's "slop chest."

THE HARPOONER AND HIS WEAPONS

Harpooners were men strong enough and brave enough to stand in the bow of an open whaleboat in heavy seas while hurling a nine-foot harpoon into the hide of a creature many times larger than the boat. The success of every whaling voyage depended on their skill and daring.

Men of Special Rank

Each ship carried three or more harpooners, one for each whaleboat. These skilled men ranked higher than seamen, and instead of sleeping in the forecastle, they shared a state room. They ate the same food the officers ate but were served separately.

Native Americans, who had lived on the New England coast long before the arrival of white settlers, were experienced hunters and harpooners. Some Native Americans became outstanding harpooners aboard Nantucket ships.

Harpoons and Lances

The harpooner's weapons were the four or five harpoons carried in each of the ship's whaleboats. Before a harpoon was thrown, it was attached to nearly 2,000 feet of line, kept neatly coiled in two wooden tubs. After the whale was harpooned, the line kept the boat connected to the whale. Sometimes, as the whale pulled against the rope, the harpoon would work loose. To keep the harpoon from pulling out, it was equipped with a special point called a "toggle iron," which tilted sideways after piercing the whale's flesh.

Each whaleboat also carried a number of lances—usually five—which were about 12 feet long. When a harpooned whale became tired and floated on the surface, one of the ship's officers killed it with a lance.

knife for cutting the rope if the whale should dive

sea anchor

identification
flag

water
keg

line tub

"THERE BLOWS!"

*I never knew why most writers of whaling stories
insist upon using the words "There she blows," because
there is no reason for saying "she" any more than "he"
and either would be a word too many. The cry was always
"There blows" with the last word long drawn out…*

—William Fish Williams, junior officer
on the whaling ship *Florence*

The cry of the lookout sent crew members scrambling
to their assigned whaleboats. The 28-foot whaleboats,
loaded with weapons, line, oars, and sails, were lowered
onto the sea. In each boat, one of the officers—the boat
header—was in charge. "Pull for your very lives," he would
shout to the oarsmen, fearing that the whale might escape.
Often crews rowed or sailed all day and night without getting
within striking distance of their prey.

Striking the Whale

As a boat approached a whale, the boat header whispered,
"Stand by your iron," and the boat steerer took up his
harpoon. The boat drew closer still until the men could hear
only the breathing of the whale and the pounding of their
hearts. When the officer commanded, "Give it the iron!" the
harpooner hurled the weapon with all his strength, piercing
the whale's hide. After that, no matter what the whale did, it
was attached to the boat. It might "sound," diving deep into
the sea, or it might "run," towing the boat through the water
on a breathtaking but dangerous trip known as a "Nantucket
sleigh ride." Occasionally boats were towed out of sight of
the main ship and were lost.

When the whale tired, the boat drew in close and the boat
header plunged his lance deep into the whale, trying to
pierce its lungs and blood vessels. Before the wounded whale
died, it would desperately thrash the water and the air with
its mighty tail, sometimes smashing the boat and throwing
men into the sea. Many whale hunters paid with their lives
for the capture of a whale.

Cutting In

After a kill, the ship became a factory whose product was whale oil. A killed whale was towed to the whaling ship and made fast alongside, its head toward the stern (rear). Working from a platform hung over the ship's side, crew members began "cutting in." They removed the whale's blubbery hide with long-handled cutting spades and knives, while using the same tools to fend off hungry sharks. The hide was removed as a single "blanket piece" of blubber, weighing about a ton. It was hauled aboard the ship with a large hook and a set of pulleys called a "block and tackle."

After being lowered into an area below the main deck, the blanket piece was cut into long strips, about a foot wide, called "horse pieces." These in turn were cut into smaller chunks, carried up onto the deck, and chopped with two-handled mincing knives. The resulting sections were called "bible leaves," because they were held together by the whale skin and looked like the pages of a book.

If many whales had been caught, this work could go on for a week. The odor of rotten meat and ankle-deep blood led one sailor to call whaling ships "floating stinkpots." Men might get only five hours of sleep each day for a week running.

Have had a very fine day. Have the whale cut in and commenced to boil. It is very fat blubber. While they were cutting in, the sharks were very thick about. I saw the men cutting them with their spades. If they cut them in the back of the neck, they will die instantly. I saw them cut a number in that way. They spun around and around, turned on their backs, and sunk out of sight. They did not get much of the whale, for the men kept fighting them off.

—Eliza Azelia Williams, wife of the
   captain of the whaling ship
   Florida, 1861

horse pieces

TRYING OUT

The bible leaves of blubber were forked into one of the boiling kettles of the tryworks—300- to 400-gallon kettles set in a brick furnace. The men often worked through the night by the eerie glow of the tryworks. To keep the fire burning, they fed it scraps of boiled-out blubber, which produced great clouds of black smoke. Workers skimmed off the whale oil as it melted out of the blubber. The oil cooled in copper tanks and then was stored in barrels.

tryworks

bible leaves

An average sperm whale produced about 40 barrels of oil. The head of a sperm whale contained a section called the "case," filled with high-grade oil that could be scooped out with buckets. The lower half of the head contained a waxy substance known as spermaceti, used for making smokeless candles. After all the oil had been extracted, the crew cleaned up the ship and left the whale carcass for the sharks.

FAMILIES AT SEA

Most whale hunters were separated from their families for years at a time, but some New England whaling captains took their families to sea with them. It was a hard life, with few of the comforts that they would have had on shore. Captains' wives lived in a rough world, surrounded by the foul smells and dirty work that were a part of whaling. Trips ashore and gams provided wives their only contact with other women.

Seagoing wives and their children learned to live with storms and dangers, but life at sea provided adventures and experiences unknown to their friends at home. Instead of going to a school, children at sea were taught reading, writing, and arithmetic by their mothers. They learned geography directly, traveling thousands of miles while children back home might never travel farther than the next town.

Stops to obtain fresh food and water gave children a chance to experience other cultures. After weeks or months of living at sea on a crowded ship, everyone aboard eagerly looked forward to these visits ashore. To New Englanders who were used to cold winters and straitlaced social customs, some of the places they visited seemed extremely exotic. In the South Pacific, islanders sometimes prepared feasts for their visitors, and sailors enjoyed evenings filled with music, dancing, and feasts of roasted pig.

"We went to an island named Ohitahoo and stayed there eight days," wrote eight-year-old Laura Jernigan in 1870. "We went to the queen's palace and she made a feast for us. Mama was the first white woman that ever was on the island. We had ten different kinds of fruits."

In English-speaking colonies, local officials would often invite the captain home for dinner. If the captain's wife was aboard, she might be introduced to the local ladies who were eager to hear of her adventures at sea. In other places, the reception might not be so friendly. Islanders sometimes attacked the whalers if they tried to come ashore.

A Baby Born at Sea

We have had an addition to the Florida's crew in the form of a little daughter, born on the 27th of February in Banderas Bay on the coast of Mexico. She weighed 6-¾ pounds, is now one month old, and weighs nine pounds. She seems very healthy and is also very quiet. We are, as may be supposed, well pleased with her. Willie is much pleased with his little sister.

—from the journal of Eliza Azelia Williams

TRAPPED IN THE ICE

By the 1870s, sperm whales had become scarce, and the New England whaling fleet began venturing into the Arctic Ocean in search of bowhead whales, a species similar to the right whale.

A New Kind of Danger

Bowhead whales were not as fierce as sperm whales, but trips into the Arctic exposed whalers to a new kind of danger. For most of the year, the cold seas there were packed with ice. Sailing ships could enter for only a few weeks in mid-summer. Even then, their crews had to keep a careful eye on the weather and the movements of floating ice.

In August 1871, fierce winds drove a floating mass of ice among a fleet of 38 whaling ships, trapping them near the northwestern shore of Alaska. As the ice piled up around the ships, the captains realized that their only hope was to abandon their vessels and try to get out aboard the five ships that remained in open water.

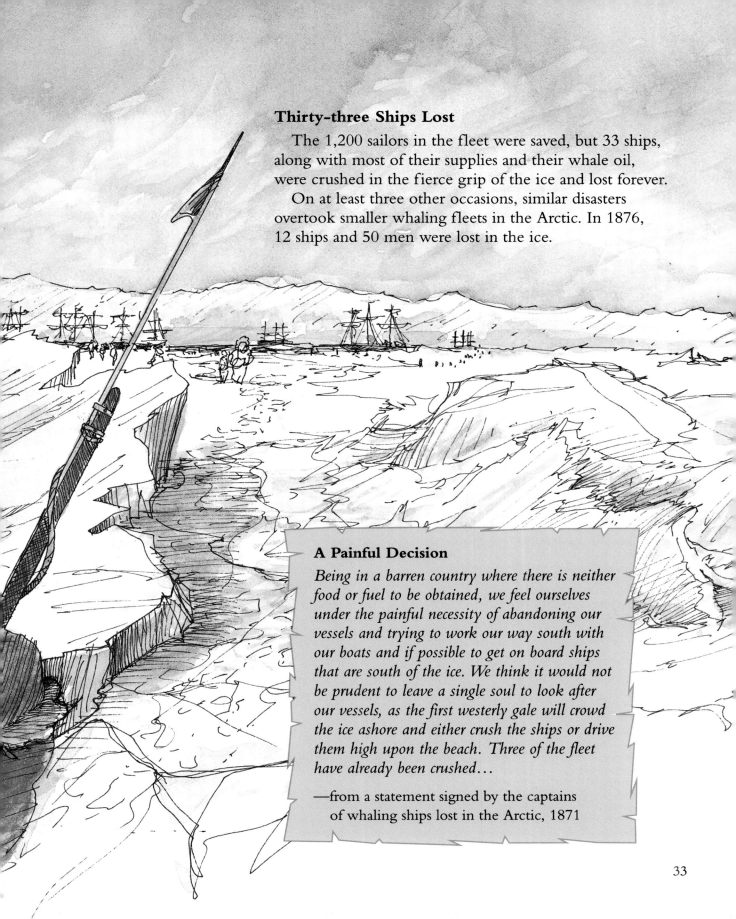

Thirty-three Ships Lost

The 1,200 sailors in the fleet were saved, but 33 ships, along with most of their supplies and their whale oil, were crushed in the fierce grip of the ice and lost forever.

On at least three other occasions, similar disasters overtook smaller whaling fleets in the Arctic. In 1876, 12 ships and 50 men were lost in the ice.

A Painful Decision

Being in a barren country where there is neither food or fuel to be obtained, we feel ourselves under the painful necessity of abandoning our vessels and trying to work our way south with our boats and if possible to get on board ships that are south of the ice. We think it would not be prudent to leave a single soul to look after our vessels, as the first westerly gale will crowd the ice ashore and either crush the ships or drive them high upon the beach. Three of the fleet have already been crushed…

—from a statement signed by the captains of whaling ships lost in the Arctic, 1871

The Tragedy of the Whaling Ship Essex

It was not uncommon for whales to smash whaleboats, but until November 20, 1820, a whale had never sunk a whaling ship. That was the fate of the whaling ship *Essex* on that date as it sailed in a vast, uncharted section of the Pacific Ocean. Twice the whale rammed the ship, striking it on both sides of its bow. Before the ship sank, the crew salvaged food and water from the wreck and set sail in three whaleboats for the coast of South America, a voyage of 3,000 miles.

Hunger and Thirst

Each of the 20 men was allowed a half pint of water and a biscuit each day. They sailed and rowed for nearly a month. Weak with hunger and nearly mad from thirst, they finally landed on an island. For four days they strengthened themselves by eating crabs, birds, and eggs. They refilled their water casks from a small spring and continued their journey, leaving three men who chose to stay on the island.

Storms separated the boats, and some men died of starvation. The others stayed alive by eating those who had died. On one of the boats, the men drew straws to determine which one of them would be killed so the others could live. Owen Coffin, a nephew of the captain, drew the short straw and was killed with a single shot from his uncle's pistol.

Two of the boats were rescued in late February near the South American coast, and a ship was sent to rescue the three men on the island. The third boat was never found. Of the original crew of 20 men, only 8 survived.

Moby Dick

Years later, a writer named Herman Melville went to sea on a whaler and met a son of Owen Chase, first mate on the *Essex*. Melville's famous novel *Moby Dick,* in which a giant white sperm whale destroys a ship, was inspired in part by the sinking of the *Essex*.

HOMEWARD BOUND

It's now we're homeward bound, my lads
And when we're done with sailing,
A winding glass around we'll pass
And damn this blubber whaling!

—from a whaling song,
"Blow Ye Winds of Morning"

Whaling captains didn't like to end their voyages until they had loaded the ship's hold with a full cargo of whale oil. If the whaling was going well, they would sometimes put into a foreign port, send their oil home on a merchant ship, and continue whaling. But finally, after three or four years, the ship would sail for home. The mood onboard was joyful as everyone looked forward to being back in their own homes with the people they loved. On shore, wives and children, mothers and fathers, eagerly awaited the ship's return.

In some New England whaling ports, captains' houses had a platform on the roof. From there, wives spent many hours watching every sail that appeared on the horizon. Sometimes wives waited in vain for ships that would never come home. For that reason, the platforms were called "widow's walks." When a returning ship was spotted and identified, the news quickly spread along the waterfront and through the town. Hundreds of people went to the wharf to welcome the crew.

When the ship had docked, husbands and wives embraced, and young children shyly said hello to fathers they often didn't recognize. Land sharks and other merchants were excited because every man onboard would soon be paid his lay, and most of them would have at least one or two hundred dollars in their pockets. Many of the men vowed they would never go whaling again. Others, who didn't know any other trade, would sign up for another voyage as soon as their money was spent.

Scrimshaw

When a voyage was over, crew members often gave gifts made from whales' teeth or whalebone to their wives, sweethearts, or friends.

These souvenirs, known as scrimshaw, were made at sea by whale hunters when they had little else to do. Making scrimshaw took skill, patience, and plenty of time. During long hours at sea, whalers created a wide variety of fancy scrimshaw. If a whaler didn't have anyone waiting for him at home, he might sell his work in a foreign port for spending money.

One common form of scrimshaw was a whale's tooth engraved with a picture of a ship, a whaling scene, or any other subject that appealed to the maker. The artist would carefully scratch the design on the surface of the tooth, then fill in the scratches with ink.

Sailors also carved useful or decorative objects from the jawbones of sperm whales and the baleen of right whales. Napkin rings, clothespins, chess pieces, and doorknobs were popular forms of scrimshaw. Some sailors used baleen to make complicated devices known as "swifts," which were used for winding yarn. Hungry sailors who yearned for the kinds of food they could get at home often made devices called "jagging wheels." After the voyage was over, the sailors' wives or sweethearts used these wheels to crimp the edges of home-baked pies.

Some sailors even made scrimshaw musical instruments. At least one musically inclined crew member made a scrimshaw banjo with parts carved from the bone and teeth of whales.

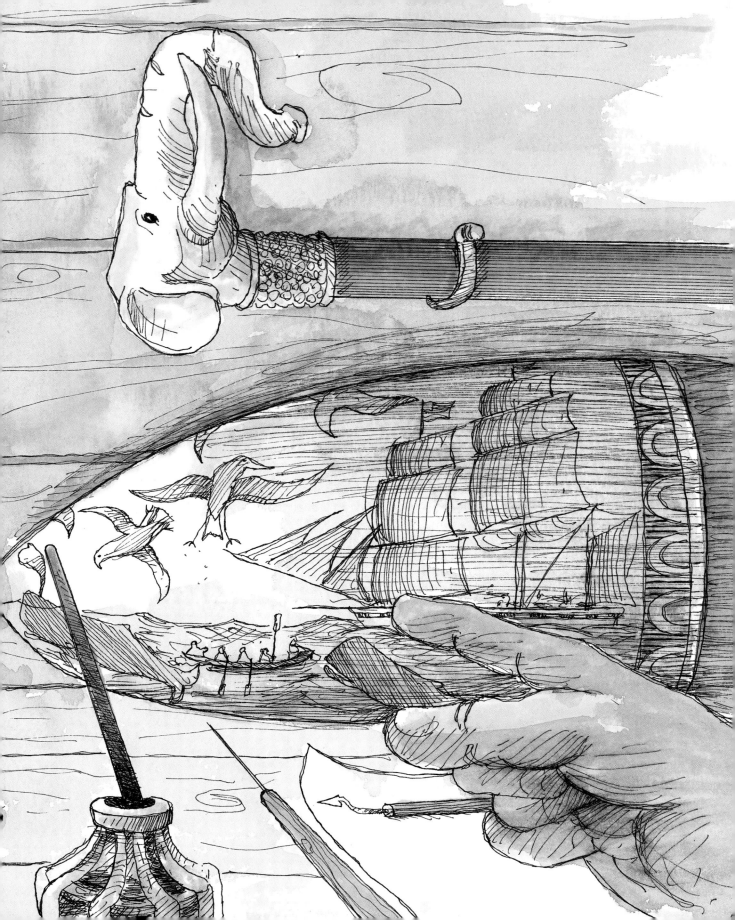

END OF AN ERA

The New England whaling industry flourished until about 1860, then went into a steady decline. There weren't enough sperm whales left to make a voyage very profitable. There were still many blue whales, fin whales, and other species, but they were fast swimmers, and sailing ships and whaleboats couldn't catch them.

Meanwhile, the discovery of petroleum in Pennsylvania was beginning to cripple the whaling industry. Petroleum was refined to produce kerosene, a cheaper lamp fuel than whale oil. For the rest of the 19th century, the demand for whale oil faded. The Yankee whaling industry faded with it.

In the early 20th century, scientists discovered new ways to use whale oil in the production of margarine, soap, and other products. Whale hunting became profitable once again, but the industry had changed. Many nations were building fleets of steel factory ships and arming them with powerful harpoon guns. The harpoons carried explosive charges that blew up deep inside the whales.

There were still a few old whaling ships afloat. They weren't fast enough to compete for blue whales, but they could still hunt for the few remaining right whales, bowheads, and sperm whales. The last New England sailing ship to venture onto the ocean in search of whales was the schooner *John R. Manta*. It made its last whaling trip in 1925 but with little success. By then, the greasy luck of Yankee whaling had finally run out.

Whaling Today

By the 1960s, the decline in the whale population caused international concern. In 1970, the United States banned the import of whale products and in 1972 banned whaling in U.S. waters. In 1985, the International Whaling Commission halted the killing of whales until populations increase. Whaling is now lawful only for Inuits and other native people with a whaling tradition, but some nations disregard IWC rules.

WHALER RECIPES

After all the fresh food was used up in the first few weeks of a voyage, whaler cooks had to find creative ways to use dried or preserved food. Here are two recipes similar to those served onboard whaling ships.

Baked Beans

2 cans red beans (15½-ounce cans)
2 teaspoons prepared mustard
4 tablespoons molasses (or 6 tablespoons brown sugar)
¼ pound salt pork (or 5 strips of bacon)
½ teaspoon salt (if bacon is used instead of salt pork)

Preheat the oven to 300 degrees. Open two cans of red beans and drain the liquid into a bowl. Mix the mustard and molasses or brown sugar into the liquid. Slice the salt pork and place about a third of the pork in the bottom of a medium-size casserole dish. (If you are using bacon, cut the slices in half and put three or four pieces into the bottom of the dish. Add ½ teaspoon salt to the liquid.) Add the beans on top of the pork. Pour the liquid over the beans. Layer the remaining pork or bacon on top of the beans. Cover and bake for 1½ hours. Then uncover the dish and bake for a final ½ hour.

Plum Duff

2 cups flour
½ teaspoon baking soda
1 teaspoon cream of tartar
1 tablespoon vegetable oil
¼ teaspoon salt

1 cup raisins
¾ cup brown sugar
¾ cup water
pancake syrup

Mix dry ingredients, including raisins and brown sugar, in a bowl. Add oil and water and mix well. Using an additional ¼ cup flour, flour your hands and add small amounts of flour to the mix as you roll meatball-size balls of dough. You should be able to make 25 to 30 balls from this recipe. Fill a large (approximately two-gallon) pot half full of water and bring it to a boil. Turn down the heat and simmer the dumplings for one hour, stirring occasionally to keep them from sticking to the bottom of the pan. Pour pancake syrup on top before serving.

WHALING SONG

"The Greenland Whale"

It was seventeen hundred and eighty-four
On March the seventeenth day,
We weighed our anchor to our bow,
And for Greenland bore away, brave boys,
And for Greenland bore away.

Bold Stevens was our captain's name,
Our ship called the Lion so bold,
And our poor souls our anchor away
To face the storms and cold, brave boys,
To face the storms and cold.

Oh, when we arrived in that cold country
Our goodly ship to moor,
We wished ourselves safe back again
With those pretty girls on shore, brave boys,
With those pretty girls on shore.

Our boatswain to the main top stand
With a spyglass in his hand,
"A whale, a whale, my lads," he cries.
"And she spouts at every span, brave boys,
And she spouts at every span."

The captain walked the quarter-deck,
And a jolly little fellow was he.
"Overhaul, overhaul your davit tackle falls,
And we'll launch our boats all three, brave boys,
And we'll launch our boats all three."

There was harpineery and lancereery
And boat steerery also,
And twelve jolly tars to tug at the oars.
And a-whaling we all go, brave boys,
And a-whaling we all go.

We struck that whale and down she went
By the flourish of her tail.
By chance we lost a man overboard
And we did not get that whale, brave boys,
And we did not get that whale.

When this news to our captain came
It grieved his heart full sore.
And for the loss of a 'prentice boy
It was half mast colors all, brave boys,
It was half mast colors all.

It's now cold months is a-coming on,
No longer can we stay here.
For the winds do blow and the whales do go,
And the daylight seldom does appear, brave boys,
And the daylight seldom does appear.

True-Life Whalers

Eliza Azelia Williams

Eliza Azelia Williams (1826–1885) was five months pregnant when she set out whaling with her husband, Thomas William Williams, captain of the *Florida*. From September 1858 to October 1861, Eliza visited every major whaling area in the world—giving birth to a son and a daughter on the way.

Though Eliza weighed less than 100 pounds, she weathered the rigors of the whaling life, choosing to go to sea rather than wait at home. She kept a journal of her travels, recording sights, sounds, and smells. Her writings give a vivid picture of everyday life aboard a whaling ship. Weather, gams with passing ships, a sailor who fell from the rigging, the death of a harpooner—all are recorded in careful detail. As much as the family livelihood depended on killing whales, she didn't relish the sight of a whale kill. She described the whales "playing about, so happy in their native element, all unconscious, it seemed, of danger. But it made me feel very bad to see them spouting blood as thick as it could be and the last struggles after they had run and sounded."

Eliza made many whaling voyages. Twice she had to abandon ship when ice-locked in the Arctic. The Williams eventually settled in California. Eliza returned to Connecticut after her husband died and was buried there in 1885.

Lewis Temple

When New England whalers met Inuit and northwestern Indian whale hunters in the mid-19th century, the clever harpoons the Native Americans had devised caused a sensation. The Native American version had a detachable head that caught in the whale's flesh at a right angle to the shaft. Such harpoons were much less likely to pull out.

Though more than a hundred patents imitated the idea, it was the solid and simple design of Lewis Temple (1800–1854), a slave-born African-American blacksmith living in New Bedford, Massachusetts, that became the harpooner's standard weapon. Though initially handmade, Temple's toggle-equipped harpoon was soon manufactured in huge quantities.

First known as "Temple's gig," the harpoon featured a curved and barbed point that pivoted on the shaft. A wooden pin the size of a matchstick held the head in line with the shaft as it penetrated the blubber. When the pin broke, it freed the head to tilt out, making the end of the harpoon T-shaped. Temple's harpoon has been described as the most important invention in the history of whaling.

Owen Chase

We have Owen Chase to thank for a detailed record of the sinking of the *Essex* and the horrific journey of its survivors (see pages 34–35). Chase, first mate on the *Essex*, had the unusual misfortune of being hit three times by the whale on that fateful day of November 20, 1820: once while in his whaleboat and twice while onboard the *Essex*.

Chase tells us that the crew salvaged three whaleboats. They set their course for Chile or Peru—3,000 miles away—instead of nearer islands, because "we feared we should be devoured by cannibals." In vivid detail, Chase describes his crew's growing desperation as food ran low. Flying fish that hit the sail were eaten uncooked, scales and all. Dolphins were often within harpooning distance, but the whalers had no harpoons with them. Barnacles found on the bottom of the boat were eaten with delight.

After nearly three months on the seas, Chase's boat separated from the others during a storm. Daily bread rations dropped to 1½ ounces, then disappeared altogether. In starving desperation, the crew resorted to cannibalism when one of their fellow crew members, Isaac Cole, died. Only eight days later, they were rescued by the brig *Indian* from London.

Chase went on to become a successful shipmaster and later a captain of the new ship *Charles Carroll*. After a final successful whaling voyage in 1840, he retired. Having faced starvation once, he made sure he was always prepared. Until he died in 1869 at the age of 73, he would often buy crackers and hide them in his attic.

Whaling Terms and their Meanings

baleen: fringed plates found in the mouths of some whales; used to strain plankton from the sea

blubber: fat on a whale just beneath its skin. Whale oil is rendered from blubber.

boat header: an officer who directs a whaleboat and, after a whale has been harpooned, kills the whale with a lance

cutting stage: the plank scaffold, suspended from the side of a whaling ship, from which crew members cut blubber from the whale

gam: a meeting of two or more ships on the high seas to exchange news, letters, and reading materials

greasy luck: successfully finding and killing whales in order to harvest whale oil

harpoon: a spear with a steel head and a wooden shaft; attached to a long line and used to pierce and hold onto a whale

lance: a steel spear used to kill a whale once it has been harpooned and is exhausted

lay: the share, based on a whaler's status and skill, received from the profits of a whaling voyage

scrimshaw: decorative or useful works of art made by sailors from the teeth or bone of whales

slop chest: a chest filled with necessary items of clothing for crew members

spermaceti: waxy matter found in the head of the sperm whale and often used for making smokeless candles

toggle iron: the pointed head of a harpoon that tilts at a right angle to the shaft, implanting itself firmly in the whale; perfected by Lewis Temple

tryworks: the brick furnace in which kettles are heated for rendering whale blubber

INDEX

Arctic Ocean, 8, 12, 32
Atlantic Ocean, 8, 17

baleen, 11, 38
barrels, 14, 15
beaked whale, 11
beluga whale, 11
bible leaves, 26, 29
blubber, 6, 16, 26, 28
blue whale, 11, 40
boat header, 25
bowhead whale, 10-11, 32

cabin boy, 8, 16
Cape Verde Islands, 17
captain, 7, 8, 16, 30, 37
carpenter, 16
case, 29
Chase, Owen, 34, 45
clothing, 20, 21
Coffin, Owen, 34
Comstock, Samuel, 7
cooper, 16
cutting in, 26

Essex, 34, 45

families, 30-31, 37, 44
fin whale, 10-11
food, 5, 21, 42

gams, 18
Globe, 7
gray whale, 10-11
greasy luck, 8, 40

harpoon, 15, 22, 44-45
harpooner, 5, 8, 16, 22, 25
humpback whale, 11

Indian Ocean, 8, 17
International Whaling
    Commission, 41
Inuit whalers, 6, 41, 44

John R. Manta, 40

killer whale, 11

lances, 15, 22, 25
land sharks, 21, 37
lay, 8, 21
lobscouse, 21

Melville, Herman, 34
Moby Dick, 34

Nantucket, 6, 7, 17, 22, 25
Native American whalers, 6,
    22, 44
New Bedford, 6, 14, 17

oil, 5, 6, 13, 28-29, 40

Pacific Ocean, 8, 30, 34
plum duff, 21, 42

right whale, 6, 10-11, 38

scrimshaw, 38
sharks, 26, 29

slop chest, 20-21
songs, 18, 43
sperm whale, 6, 11, 29, 32, 38,
    40
spermaceti, 29

Temple, Lewis, 44-45
toggle iron, 22, 44-45
tryworks, 13, 28-29

watch, 19
whaleboat, 12-13, 22-23, 25,
    34
widow's walks, 37
Williams, Eliza Azelia, 26, 31,
    44

Robert F. Baldwin of Newcastle, Maine, and Des Moines, Iowa, has spent much of his life on or near the ocean. His articles and short stories about the sea and the people who work on it have appeared in such magazines as *Sea Frontiers, Offshore, Down East, New Bedford, New Hampshire Profiles, Traditional Home,* and *Yankee.* This is his first book for young readers.

Richard Erickson graduated from Atlanta's Portfolio Center in 1989. A native of Chicago, he currently lives in the North Georgia mountains with his wife, Kathy, two sons, four dogs, and three cats.